THE SECRET THOUGHTS OF
BIRDS

THE SECRET THOUGHTS

OF

BIRDS

BY
CJ Rose

THE
collective
BOOK STUDIO

For the last time, Paul, we are not going to fly in a "P" formation.

We are "lovebirds"
in name only. . . .
We find each other
absolutely intolerable.

If you so much as touch one more egg, man ape, you're going down.

Okay, maybe that sparrow was right. This thing on the top of my head is kind of weird looking.

You are wrong on both counts:
I don't want a cracker, and my name's not "Polly."

Fred, I just want to reiterate one last time the dire circumstances that befall those who don't share.

My favorite hobby?
Watching birdwatchers.
And yours?

All my plans for world conquest are slowly but surely falling into place. . . .

Well I say you're wrong and that smaller beaks *are* better.

So, you're seriously telling me that all six of us forgot to bring shampoo?

I *am* a little hungry, but that is a very aggressive-looking rabbit. . . .

Did you seriously eat *all* the sunflower seeds again, Larry?

**Any more
wood-peckering
today, and I am going
to need an aspirin.**

I know I'm supposed to be the national bird of America and everything, but I'm actually Canadian.

Oh, there you are!
I was wondering
why my feet were
so warm.

I will probably return to Capistrano this year with the other swallows . . . but I have to say, it's getting a little old.

Oh, so you think I'm a "hairy chicken," huh? Come a little closer, so I can teach you all about the Kiwi Bird Karate Kick!

Mom, can you show me how you fly backwards again? It's the coolest!

Why do we stand like this? 'Cause standing on two legs is bad luck, that's why!

Hey, that's the same story with me. Everyone said I was unattractive as a kid, but then I just blossomed!

When will I sing?
Right after you
whip up a bowl of
sunflower seeds
and some fresh
newspaper, Bub.

Is that cat seriously trying to sneak up on me again?

Not that I don't like hanging with you guys, but this would be a way better party if there were some girls here.

And here comes
the farmer to
pointlessly put up his
scarecrow again.

I am going to take an extra moment to marvel at your rare beauty. And then I am going to gobble you up!

Hey, I am *not* mocking you! I think that the term "mimicking with improvement" is a more accurate description.

Ok, let's practice again. Two steps forward, then a right spin turn, and then we belt out the triple gobble. Keep it tight.

Well, I was really hoping for more of a Victorian look, but this will have to do.

"I'm a blackbird singing in the morning sun." Hey, that's catchy!

Hey Ma,
I could use a
snack back here.

Oh, yeah? Well I once fit a whole whale in my throat pouch. Beat that!

Shall we top off this romantic evening by poop-bombing some humans on the boardwalk?

Basset hound boogers are just so yum!

Last one out's a rotten egg! Wait . . . bad metaphor. Sorry!

Flee, flee, before my majestic form, small rodents of the field!

I am seriously
considering a nose job.

The idea of burying my head in the sand to hide from danger is ridiculous. Instead, I just close my eyes, and that turns me invisible!

Oh, that's just great. The human is late with my nectar refill yet again.

Well I guess this officially makes me the "early bird!"

And that's essentially how the third law of thermodynamics works in regards to entropy.
Any questions?

Ah, finally finished the nest! Now I just need to figure out where that smoky smell is coming from.

Yeah, frankly I'm not sure why we don't get electrocuted either.

That whole "flying south for the winter" thing is starting to make a bit more sense.

It's weird, but I seemingly get more gorgeous with each passing day.

That must be a human. I heard that you can identify them by the small metal box that they hold in their hand and constantly stare at.

Ok, life is officially pretty good for us birds.

Wanna go circle over some humans and freak them out?

I wonder if anyone will notice if I pee in here?

When you got it, flaunt it!

Stop giving me the silent treatment!

No, Russell, I don't want to hear your classic, owl-themed knock-knock joke again.

Honey, my sixth sense is telling me that we should just stay in the house today.

Look deeply into my eyes, human. Feel your fingers relaxing and your hand gently dropping that bologna sandwich onto the ground.

Well, if you put it
that way, then yes,
we can be pals!

Copyright © 2022 Steelhead Book Services, LTD.

Library of Congress catalog in Publication data is available.

ISBN 978-1-68555-010-3
Ebook ISBN: 978-1-68555-011-0
LCCN 2021951822

Printed and bound in China by
Reliance Printing Company Limited, Shenzhen.

Cover and interior design by AJ Hansen.
All images courtesy of Shutterstock.

1 3 5 7 9 10 8 6 4 2

The Collective Book Studio®
Oakland, California
www.thecollectivebook.studio